The Life and Ministry of
JESUS CHRIST

The Beginning

NAVPRESS
BRINGING TRUTH TO LIFE
NavPress Publishing Group
P.O. Box 35001, Colorado Springs, Colorado 80935

OUR GUARANTEE TO YOU

We believe so strongly in the message of our books that we are making this quality guarantee to you. If for any reason you are disappointed with the content of this book, return the title page to us with your name and address and we will refund to you the list price of the book. To help us serve you better, please briefly describe why you were disappointed. Mail your refund request to: NavPress, P.O. Box 35002, Colorado Springs, CO 80935.

The Navigators is an international Christian organization. Our mission is to reach, disciple, and equip people to know Christ and to make Him known through successive generations. We envision multitudes of diverse people in the United States and every other nation who have a passionate love for Christ, live a lifestyle of sharing Christ's love, and multiply spiritual laborers among those without Christ.

NavPress is the publishing ministry of The Navigators. NavPress publications help believers learn biblical truth and apply what they learn to their lives and ministries. Our mission is to stimulate spiritual formation among our readers.

© 1996 by The Navigators
All rights reserved. No part of this publication may be reproduced in any form without written permission from NavPress, P.O. Box 35001, Colorado Springs, CO 80935.
www.navpress.com
ISBN 08910-99654

Cover illustration: Planet Art
Map: GeoSystems Global Corporation

This series was produced for NavPress with the assistance of The Livingstone Corporation. James C. Galvin, Valerie Weidemann, and Daryl J. Lucas, project editors.

Unless otherwise identified, all Scripture quotations in this publication are taken from the *HOLY BIBLE: NEW INTERNATIONAL VERSION* ® (NIV®). Copyright © 1973, 1978, 1984 by International Bible Society. Used by permission of Zondervan Publishing House. Another version used is the *New American Standard Bible* (NASB), © The Lockman Foundation 1960, 1962, 1963, 1968, 1971, 1972, 1973, 1975, 1977.

Printed in the United States of America

4 5 6 7 8 9 10 11 12 13 14 15 16 / 07 06 05 04 03 02 01

FOR A FREE CATALOG OF
NAVPRESS BOOKS & BIBLE STUDIES,
CALL 1-800-366-7788 (USA)
or 1-416-499-4615 (CANADA)

CONTENTS

Study guides in the
LIFE AND MINISTRY OF JESUS CHRIST series:

INTRODUCTION

If you want to learn more about Jesus Christ and become more like Him, then THE LIFE AND MINISTRY OF JESUS CHRIST series is for you and your small group. This seven-book Bible study spans all four Gospels, covers the entire life of Christ in chronological order, and emphasizes personal application of biblical truth. By using an inductive study format, THE LIFE AND MINISTRY OF JESUS CHRIST helps you investigate for yourself what Jesus did and what He taught.

Each guide has five lessons and may be studied in five sessions, or in as many as ten to twelve sessions if your group prefers a slower pace. For best results, each group member should study the passages listed and write out the answers to the questions—including the application questions in the side columns. Then, as you meet with your Bible study group or class you can discuss what you have observed and applied. Use the side columns to write out any additional insights or applications that emerge from the discussion. The emphasis on application helps to maintain a balance between factual knowledge and character development. The more time and prayer you invest in the study, the more you will gain from it.

In each section of a given lesson, one biblical passage will be the main focus of study. That passage is printed out for you. Additional passages may also be listed. Read them as you have time.

A separate leader's resource guide is available for THE LIFE AND MINISTRY OF JESUS CHRIST series that provides additional background for each lesson and optional discussion questions for the group.

The Scripture passages were arranged based on the order presented by A. T. Robertson in *A Harmony of the Gospels* (Harper & Brothers, 1950). A harmony is a sequencing of the four Gospel accounts of the life of Jesus in parallel form to facilitate a study of His life and ministry. You can find the harmony used in this study in the "Harmony of the Life and Ministry of Jesus Christ" in the back of each study guide.

A harmony shows the events in the life of Christ in chronological order. Some events, such as the feeding of the five thousand, are recorded in all four Gospels; others, such as Jesus' interview with Nicodemus in the Gospel of John, appear in only one. Mark's Gospel is the most chronological; Matthew's follows themes more closely than chronology.

Without careful study and the aid of a harmony, the Gospels may appear to contain chronological discrepancies. The order of the material in each Gospel differs because Jesus taught the same truths, told the same parables, and performed similar miracles many times in His three-and-a-half year ministry. So Matthew recorded the contents of the Sermon on the Mount in one large section toward the beginning of Jesus' ministry (Matthew 5–7), while Luke wrote down similar teachings of Jesus throughout His ministry (Luke 6:17-49, 11:1-13, 13:22-30). Undoubtedly Jesus pronounced judgment on those who opposed and harassed Him a number of times, so Matthew tells of an incident in Galilee toward the middle of His ministry (Matthew 12:22-45) while Luke records another such confrontation, this time in Judea, later in His ministry (Luke 11:14-36). These are not contradictions but records of similar events.

This Bible study resulted from the diligent work of many men and women around the world. A team of Navigator staff realized the need for this study and began putting it together. Others field tested the material and made refinements. Still others read it and offered valuable advice. Then skilled editors shaped the study to its final form.

To all who have prayed and labored diligently, a hearty word of thanks. It is, in every sense, the result of a team effort, coached and coordinated by the Holy Spirit. As the Author of the Word of God, as Teacher and Interpreter of the Word to believers, and as the Divine Distributor of His gifts to them, the Holy Spirit has in a unique way directed the production of this study. His desire for its effectiveness must stem from His special ministry of revealing and glorifying Jesus Christ in our lives. To this purpose the study is dedicated.

> *"I have much more to say to you, more than you can now bear. But when he, the Spirit of truth, comes, he will guide you into all truth. He will not speak on his own; he will speak only what he hears, and he will tell you what is yet to come. He will bring glory to me by taking from what is mine and making it known to you. All that belongs to the Father is mine. That is why I said the Spirit will take from what is mine and make it known to you." (John 16:12-15)*

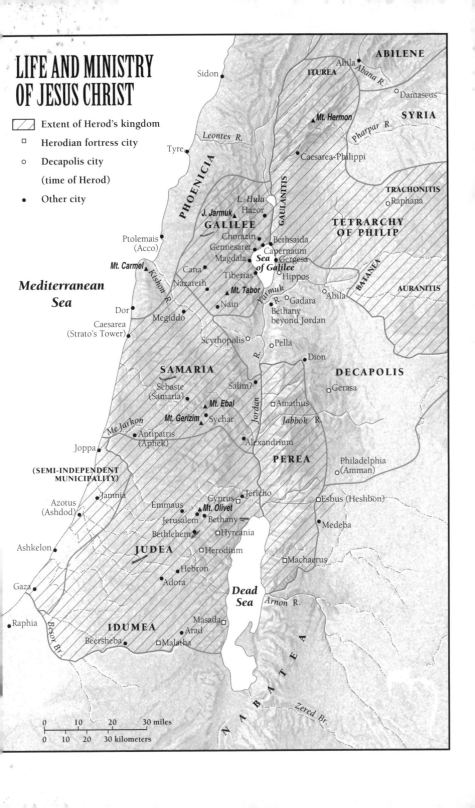

LIFE AND MINISTRY
OF JESUS CHRIST

⧅	Extent of Herod's kingdom
☐	Herodian fortress city
○	Decapolis city
	(time of Herod)
●	Other city

ABILENE

Sidon

ITUREA

Abila
Abana R.

Damascus

SYRIA

▲ Mt. Hermon

Leontes R.

Tyre

PHOENICIA

Pharpar R.

Caesarea-Philippi

TRACHONITIS

Raphana

L. Hula

J. Jarmuk ▲   Hazor

GALILEE

GAULANITIS

TETRARCHY
OF PHILIP

Ptolemais
(Acco)

Chorazin
Gennesaret
Magdala
Cana
Nazareth
Tiberias

Bethsaida
Capernaum
Sea
of Galilee
Gergesa
Hippos

BATANEA

AURANITIS

Mt. Carmel ▲

Kishon R.

▲ Mt. Tabor

Nain

Yarmuk R.

Gadara

Abila

Mediterranean
Sea

Dor

Caesarea
(Strato's Tower)

Megiddo

Scythopolis

Bethany
beyond Jordan

Pella

Dion

DECAPOLIS

SAMARIA

Sebaste
(Samaria)

Salim?

Gerasa

▲ Mt. Ebal
Mt. Gerizim ▲   Sychar

Me Jarkon

Antipatris
(Aphek)

Jordan R.

Amathus

Jabbok R.

Joppa

Alexandrium

PEREA

Philadelphia
(Amman)

(SEMI-INDEPENDENT
MUNICIPALITY)

Jamnia

Azotus
(Ashdod)

Emmaus

Cyprus   Jericho

▲ Mt. Olivet
Jerusalem   Bethany
Bethlehem

Esbus (Heshbon)

Medeba

Ashkelon

Hyrcania

JUDEA

Herodium

Machaerus

Gaza

Hebron
Adora

Dead
Sea

Arnon R.

Raphia

Besor Br.

Masada
Arad

IDUMEA

N
A
B
A
T
E
A

Beersheba   Malatha

Zered Br.

0	10	20	30 miles	
0	10	20	30 kilometers	

LESSON ONE
THE TRUTH ABOUT JESUS

More has been written about Jesus of Nazareth than any other person in history. The story of His life is compelling, and His teaching demands a response. A look at Jesus through the eyes of the four Gospel writers will encourage you to give serious consideration to His claims. This lesson will introduce you to the authors of the four Gospels and will help you understand how Jesus' message is relevant today.

In the past God spoke to our fore-fathers through the prophets at many times and in various ways, but in these last days he has spoken to us by his Son, whom he appointed heir of all things, and through whom he made the universe. (Hebrews 1:1-2)

THE MEN WHO WROTE THE GOSPELS
Mark 1:1, Luke 1:1-4

1Many have undertaken to draw up an account of the things that have been fulfilled among us, 2just as they were handed down to us by those who from the first were eyewitnesses and servants of the word. 3Therefore, since I myself have carefully investigated everything from the beginning, it seemed good also to me to write an orderly account for you, most excellent Theophilus, 4so that you may know the certainty of the things you have been taught. (Luke 1:1-4)

As you study the life of Jesus, you will discover that each of the four Gospels presents a different

9

viewpoint. Each Gospel writer, pursuing his own theme, chose to record only certain events from Jesus' life and ministry. Each author had a different relationship to Jesus and a unique purpose for writing his narrative.

What one question about Jesus Christ would you like answered by your study of the Gospels?

1. What experience or credentials do each of the Gospel writers have to back up the credibility of their stories?

   Matthew (see Matthew 9:9-13)

   Tax collector = Conversion = follow me! disciples writing to Jews - Jesus Christ is the messiah

   Mark (see Acts 12:23–13:13, 2 Timothy 4:11)

   John Barnabas accompany Paul on journey - 1st trip he left. - Paul refers as profitably now. 1st of 4 gospels written wrote the - Romans (Gentiles) - showed Je as servant

   Luke (see Luke 1:1-4, Acts 1:1-3)

   Physician - author of Luke + acts Contemporary of Paul may have been then companion of Christ Good Historian - Talks about shows Jesus as son of God (story of Jesus)

   John (see Mark 1:19-20, John 21:20-25)

   Fisherman - Peter Andrew - portrays Jesus as God

10

2. Why is assurance of accuracy so important
   for the Gospels?

Salvation depends on it

3. How do the opening words of each Gospel
   help explain the author's purpose in writing?

4. What impact do you think the Gospel writers wanted their books to have on their
   readers?

How would you
like your relation-
ship with Christ
to be different as a
result of studying
His life and
ministry?

GOD BECAME A HUMAN BEING
John 1:1-18

[1]In the beginning was the Word, and the Word was with God, and the Word was God. [2]He was with God in the beginning.

[3]Through him all things were made; without him nothing was made that has been made. [4]In him was life, and that life was the light of men. [5]The light shines in the darkness, but the darkness has not understood it.

[6]There came a man who was sent from God; his name was John. [7]He came as a witness to testify concerning that light, so that through him all men might believe. [8]He himself was not the light; he came only as a witness to the light. [9]The true light that gives light to every man was coming into the world.

[10]He was in the world, and though the world was made through him, the world did not recognize him. [11]He came to that which was his own, but his own did not receive him. [12]Yet to all who received him, to those who believed in his name, he gave the right to become children of God—[13]children born not of natural descent, nor of human decision or a husband's will, but born of God.

[14]The Word became flesh and made his dwelling among us. We have seen his glory, the glory of the One and Only, who came from the Father, full of grace and truth.

[15]John testifies concerning him. He cries out, saying, "This was he of whom I said, 'He who comes after me has surpassed me because he was before me.'" [16]From the fullness of his grace we have all received one blessing after another. [17]For the law was given through Moses; grace and truth came through Jesus Christ. [18]No one has ever seen God, but God the One and Only, who is at the Father's side, has made him known. (John 1:1-18)

The Gospel of John clearly shows us that Jesus was both fully God and fully man. Even while

Jesus lived on earth, He was the Eternal Son of God who has always existed. Because Jesus is God's Son, He is able to clearly and accurately show us what God is like.

5. According to John, who is the Word?

God is the word

6. Why did Jesus become a human being and live among us?

Live and died that we might salvation.

7. Why do you think John presents Jesus in this way (John 20:31)?

In what practical way can you welcome Christ into your life?

8. How can a person receive Jesus Christ?

THE ANCESTORS OF JESUS
Matthew 1:1-17, Luke 3:23-38

¹*A record of the genealogy of Jesus Christ the son of David, the son of Abraham:*

²*Abraham was the father of Isaac,*
   Isaac the father of Jacob,
   Jacob the father of Judah and his brothers,
³*Judah the father of Perez and Zerah, whose mother was Tamar,*
Perez the father of Hezron,
Hezron the father of Ram,
⁴*Ram the father of Amminadab,*
Amminadab the father of Nahshon,
Nahshon the father of Salmon,
⁵*Salmon the father of Boaz, whose mother was Rahab,*
Boaz the father of Obed, whose mother was Ruth,
Obed the father of Jesse,
⁶*and Jesse the father of King David.*
David was the father of Solomon, whose mother had been Uriah's wife,
⁷*Solomon the father of Rehoboam,*
Rehoboam the father of Abijah,
Abijah the father of Asa,
⁸*Asa the father of Jehoshaphat,*
Jehoshaphat the father of Jehoram,
Jehoram the father of Uzziah,
⁹*Uzziah the father of Jotham,*
Jotham the father of Ahaz,
Ahaz the father of Hezekiah,
¹⁰*Hezekiah the father of Manasseh,*
Manasseh the father of Amon,
Amon the father of Josiah,
¹¹*and Josiah the father of Jeconiah and his brothers at the time of the exile to Babylon.*

¹²*After the exile to Babylon:*
Jeconiah was the father of Shealtiel,
Shealtiel the father of Zerubbabel,
¹³*Zerubbabel the father of Abiud,*
Abiud the father of Eliakim,

Eliakim the father of Azor,
¹⁴Azor the father of Zadok,
Zadok the father of Akim,
Akim the father of Eliud,
¹⁵Eliud the father of Eleazar,
Eleazar the father of Matthan,
Matthan the father of Jacob,
¹⁶and Jacob the father of Joseph, the husband of
*   Mary, of whom was born Jesus, who is*
*   called Christ.*

¹⁷Thus there were fourteen generations in all
from Abraham to David, fourteen from David to
the exile to Babylon, and fourteen from the exile to
the Christ. (Matthew 1:1-17)

Matthew wrote his Gospel primarily to the Jews, who were waiting for the Messiah. To prove that Jesus fulfilled the Old Testament prophecies about the Messiah, Matthew began his Gospel with a genealogy. This family history shows that Jesus was a descendant of Abraham, who was the father of all Jews, and a direct descendant of David, just as the prophets had predicted.

9. What are the backgrounds of the five women mentioned in Matthew's genealogy?

Tamar (see Genesis 38:15-30)

Rahab (see Joshua 2:1-24, 6:21-25)

Ruth (see Ruth 1:1-19, 4:13-17)

moabite

Bathsheba (see 2 Samuel 11)

Mary (see Luke 1:26-38)

virgin mother

How should the reality that God became a human being affect your life today?

10. Why do you think these women were included in Matthew's genealogy?

11. How do family histories affect who we are?

12. What can we learn from this genealogy about how God works through people and history?

How do you want to respond to the truth you learn about Christ in this study?

Each of the Gospel writers paints a unique picture of Christ, yet one message is clearly communicated: Jesus is the long-awaited Messiah. He left Heaven and became a human being in order to save us from our sins. We must accept this truth about Jesus if we hope to trust our eternal future to Him.

LESSON TWO
BREAKING THE SILENCE

God had not spoken through angels or prophets for more than four hundred years. Jews all over the world were waiting for Him to break this strange silence with news of the expected Messiah. The Gospel of Luke describes to us how angels delivered promises from God that would fulfill the words of the prophets. The "time had fully come" and the Messiah (Jesus Christ) and His forerunner (John the Baptist) were about to appear. This lesson will show you how God used ordinary, but faithful, people to bring about His plan of salvation for the world.

> *But when the time had fully come, God sent his Son, born of a woman, born under law, to redeem those under law, that we might receive the full rights of sons.*
> (Galatians 4:4-5)

AN ANGEL PROMISES THE BIRTH OF JOHN TO ZECHARIAH *Luke 1:5-25*

⁵In the time of Herod king of Judea there was a priest named Zechariah, who belonged to the priestly division of Abijah; his wife Elizabeth was also a descendant of Aaron. ⁶Both of them were upright in the sight of God, observing all the Lord's commandments and regulations blamelessly. ⁷But they had no children, because Elizabeth was barren; and they were both well along in years.

⁸Once when Zechariah's division was on duty and he was serving as priest before God, ⁹he was chosen by lot, according to the custom of the priest-hood, to go into the temple of the Lord and burn incense. [10]And when the time for the burning of incense came, all the assembled worshipers were praying outside.

[11]Then an angel of the Lord appeared to him, standing at the right side of the altar of incense. [12]When Zechariah saw him, he was startled and was gripped with fear. [13]But the angel said to him: "Do not be afraid, Zechariah; your prayer has been heard. Your wife Elizabeth will bear you a son, and you are to give him the name John. [14]He will be a joy and delight to you, and many will rejoice because of his birth, [15]for he will be great in the sight of the Lord. He is never to take wine or other fermented drink, and he will be filled with the Holy Spirit even from birth. [16]Many of the people of Israel will he bring back to the Lord their God. [17]And he will go on before the Lord, in the spirit and power of Elijah, to turn the hearts of the fathers to their children and the disobedient to the wisdom of the righteous—to make ready a people prepared for the Lord."

[18]Zechariah asked the angel, "How can I be sure of this? I am an old man and my wife is well along in years."

[19]The angel answered, "I am Gabriel. I stand in the presence of God, and I have been sent to speak to you and to tell you this good news. [20]And now you will be silent and not able to speak until the day this happens, because you did not believe my words, which will come true at their proper time."

[21]Meanwhile, the people were waiting for Zechariah and wondering why he stayed so long in the temple. [22]When he came out, he could not speak to them. They realized he had seen a vision in the temple, for he kept making signs to them but remained unable to speak.

[23]When his time of service was completed, he returned home. [24]After this his wife Elizabeth became pregnant and for five months remained in seclusion. [25]"The Lord has done this for me," she

said. "In these days he has shown his favor and taken away my disgrace among the people."
(Luke 1:5-25)

Zechariah and his wife, Elizabeth, were old and childless. Barrenness was considered to be a great shame in Jewish culture—a sign of the absence of God's blessing. But God chose to work through their impossible situation to bring about the fulfillment of all the prophecies concerning the Messiah.

1. How did Zechariah and Elizabeth handle the pain of childlessness?

2. What unusual things would their promised son accomplish?

What holds you back from believing that God could do something amazing through your life?

3. How do you think Zechariah and Elizabeth felt during this time?

● ●

AN ANGEL PROMISES THE BIRTH OF JESUS TO MARY *Luke 1:26-38*

[26]In the sixth month, God sent the angel Gabriel to Nazareth, a town in Galilee, [27]to a virgin pledged to be married to a man named Joseph, a descendant of David. The virgin's name was Mary. [28]The angel went to her and said, "Greetings, you who are highly favored! The Lord is with you."

[29]Mary was greatly troubled at his words and wondered what kind of greeting this might be. [30]But the angel said to her, "Do not be afraid, Mary, you have found favor with God. [31]You will be with child and give birth to a son, and you are to give him the name Jesus. [32]He will be great and will be called the Son of the Most High. The Lord God will give him the throne of his father David, [33]and he will reign over the house of Jacob forever; his kingdom will never end."

[34]"How will this be," Mary asked the angel, "since I am a virgin?"

[35]The angel answered, "The Holy Spirit will come upon you, and the power of the Most High will overshadow you. So the holy one to be born will be called the Son of God. [36]Even Elizabeth your relative is going to have a child in her old age,

and she who was said to be barren is in her sixth month. ³⁷For nothing is impossible with God."

³⁸"I am the Lord's servant," Mary answered. "May it be to me as you have said." Then the angel left her. (Luke 1:26-38)

Mary, a poor, young girl from Nazareth, was not the obvious choice to be the mother of the Messiah! But God chose her for this amazing privilege because He knew she had a willing and humble heart.

4. What characteristics did Mary have in common with Zechariah and Elizabeth?

5. What does Mary's response to the angel tell us about the kind of responses God desires from us?

What frustrations or personal doubts can you identify in your life that need to be entrusted to God?

6. In what practical ways does God want to work through us today?

23

MARY VISITS ELIZABETH
Luke 1:39-56

[39]At that time Mary got ready and hurried to a town in the hill country of Judea, [40]where she entered Zechariah's home and greeted Elizabeth. [41]When Elizabeth heard Mary's greeting, the baby leaped in her womb, and Elizabeth was filled with the Holy Spirit. [42]In a loud voice she exclaimed: "Blessed are you among women, and blessed is the child you will bear! [43]But why am I so favored, that the mother of my Lord should come to me? [44]As soon as the sound of your greeting reached my ears, the baby in my womb leaped for joy. [45]Blessed is she who has believed that what the Lord has said to her will be accomplished!"

[46]And Mary said:

*"My soul glorifies the Lord
    [47]and my spirit rejoices in God my Savior,
[48]for he has been mindful
        of the humble state of his servant.
From now on all generations will call me blessed,
    [49]for the Mighty One has done great things for
        me—
    holy is his name.
[50]His mercy extends to those who fear him,
    from generation to generation.
[51]He has performed mighty deeds with his arm;
    he has scattered those who are proud in their
        inmost thoughts.
[52]He has brought down rulers from their
        thrones
    but has lifted up the humble.
[53]He has filled the hungry with good things
    but has sent the rich away empty.
[54]He has helped his servant Israel,
    remembering to be merciful
[55]to Abraham and his descendants forever,
    even as he said to our fathers."*

[56]Mary stayed with Elizabeth for about three months and then returned home. (Luke 1:39-56)

The unusual experiences of both Mary and Elizabeth created a special relationship between them. Elizabeth's wisdom and courage strengthened Mary's faith, as she probably wondered if her memory of the angel's visit was real. Elizabeth, who faced the discomfort of being pregnant in her old age, must have appreciated Mary's help and companionship.

7. What is significant about Elizabeth's greeting to Mary?

8. How did Mary and Elizabeth support each other during this time?

How could you apply what you have learned from this story to your relationship with a friend or family member?

9. What lessons about friendship can we learn from Mary and Elizabeth?

JOHN THE BAPTIST IS BORN
Luke 1:57-80

⁵⁷When it was time for Elizabeth to have her baby, she gave birth to a son. ⁵⁸Her neighbors and relatives heard that the Lord had shown her great mercy, and they shared her joy.

⁵⁹On the eighth day they came to circumcise the child, and they were going to name him after his father Zechariah, ⁶⁰but his mother spoke up and said, "No! He is to be called John."

⁶¹They said to her, "There is no one among your relatives who has that name."

⁶²Then they made signs to his father, to find out what he would like to name the child. ⁶³He asked for a writing tablet, and to everyone's astonishment he wrote, "His name is John." ⁶⁴Immediately his mouth was opened and his tongue was loosed, and he began to speak, praising God. ⁶⁵The neighbors were all filled with awe, and throughout the hill country of Judea people were talking about all these things. ⁶⁶Everyone who heard this wondered about it, asking, "What then is this child going to be?" For the Lord's hand was with him.

⁶⁷His father Zechariah was filled with the Holy Spirit and prophesied:

⁶⁸"Praise be to the Lord, the God of Israel,
>   because he has come and has redeemed his
>   people.
⁶⁹He has raised up a horn of salvation for us
>   in the house of his servant David
⁷⁰(as he said through his holy prophets of long
>   ago),
⁷¹salvation from our enemies
>   and from the hand of all who hate us—
⁷²to show mercy to our fathers
>   and to remember his holy covenant,
>   ⁷³the oath he swore to our father Abraham:
⁷⁴to rescue us from the hand of our enemies,
>   and to enable us to serve him without fear

*75*in holiness and righteousness before him all
        our days.
*76*And you, my child, will be called a prophet of
        the Most High;
    for you will go on before the Lord to prepare
        the way for him,
*77*to give his people the knowledge of salvation
        through the forgiveness of their sins,
*78*because of the tender mercy of our God,
    by which the rising sun will come to us from
        heaven
*79*to shine on those living in darkness
    and in the shadow of death,
to guide our feet into the path of peace."

*80*And the child grew and became strong in
spirit; and he lived in the desert until he appeared
publicly to Israel. (Luke 1:57-80)

Imagine the joy surrounding John's birth! After
years of suffering the shame of childlessness,
Zechariah and Elizabeth were blessed with a son
who would prepare the way for the Messiah. In
obedience to the angel's instructions, the proud
parents named their son John, which means
"God has been gracious."

10. Why do you think God wanted the child to
    be named John? (See Luke 1:13.)

What attitude or characteristic do you see in the life of Zechariah, Elizabeth, or Mary that you want to cultivate in your own life?

11. How did Zechariah and Elizabeth's friends
    and neighbors react to the birth of John?

What practical
steps could you
take today to allow
God to work
through you?

12. What can we learn from Zechariah about
    passing on our faith to our children?

Both Elizabeth and Mary understood that God
had chosen them to be part of a special plan. As
they anticipated the fulfillment of God's
promises to them, they must have marveled at
His decision to use them. Just as God used faithful people to fulfill His plan of salvation for the
world, He wants to work through us to accomplish His will today.

LESSON THREE
A BLESSING FROM GOD

✛

Every child is special and a blessing from God. But the Gospels tell us about a baby who was born to be a blessing for the whole world—He was the Son of God. Of all four Gospel writers, Luke gives us the most detail surrounding this awesome occasion. By studying Jesus' birth, development, and childhood, this lesson will help you renew your enthusiasm to live for Him.

Therefore the LORD himself will give you a sign: The virgin will be with child and will give birth to a son, and will call him Immanuel.
(Isaiah 7:14)

AN ANGEL APPEARS TO JOSEPH
Matthew 1:18-25

18This is how the birth of Jesus Christ came about: His mother Mary was pledged to be married to Joseph, but before they came together, she was found to be with child through the Holy Spirit. 19Because Joseph her husband was a righteous man and did not want to expose her to public disgrace, he had in mind to divorce her quietly.

20But after he had considered this, an angel of the Lord appeared to him in a dream and said, "Joseph son of David, do not be afraid to take Mary home as your wife, because what is conceived in her is from the Holy Spirit. 21She will give birth to a son, and you are to give him the name Jesus, because he will save his people from their sins."

[22]All this took place to fulfill what the Lord had said through the prophet: [23]"The virgin will be with child and will give birth to a son, and they will call him Immanuel"—which means, "God with us."

[24]When Joseph woke up, he did what the angel of the Lord had commanded him and took Mary home as his wife. [25]But he had no union with her until she gave birth to a son. And he gave him the name Jesus. (Matthew 1:18-25)

Joseph, engaged to Mary, discovered to his dismay that she was expecting a child. Even though Joseph had the legal right to divorce Mary, he chose to obey the angel's command to marry her. He wisely followed God's guidance, even when it required giving up his own rights and risking public humiliation.

1. What character qualities did Joseph demonstrate?

Obedience
Compassion - Love
studied before angel

2. What options were available to Joseph in this situation? (See Deuteronomy 22:23-27.)

Divorce or Marry
Death

3. What influenced Joseph's final decision?

angeli command

4. How does our desire for acceptance keep us from making wise decisions?

What personal desires or rights do you need to give up to better obey God?

• •

JESUS IS BORN
Luke 2:1-20

¹In those days Caesar Augustus issued a decree that a census should be taken of the entire Roman world. ²(This was the first census that took place while Quirinius was governor of Syria.) ³And everyone went to his own town to register.

⁴So Joseph also went up from the town of Nazareth in Galilee to Judea, to Bethlehem the town of David, because he belonged to the house and line of David. ⁵He went there to register with Mary, who was pledged to be married to him and was expecting a child. ⁶While they were there, the

31

time came for the baby to be born, [7]and she gave birth to her firstborn, a son. She wrapped him in cloths and placed him in a manger, because there was no room for them in the inn.

[8]And there were shepherds living out in the fields nearby, keeping watch over their flocks at night. [9]An angel of the Lord appeared to them, and the glory of the Lord shone around them, and they were terrified. [10]But the angel said to them, "Do not be afraid. I bring you good news of great joy that will be for all the people. [11]Today in the town of David a Savior has been born to you; he is Christ the Lord. [12]This will be a sign to you: You will find a baby wrapped in cloths and lying in a manger."

[13]Suddenly a great company of the heavenly host appeared with the angel, praising God and saying,

[14]"Glory to God in the highest,
and on earth peace to men on whom his favor rests."

[15]When the angels had left them and gone into heaven, the shepherds said to one another, "Let's go to Bethlehem and see this thing that has happened, which the Lord has told us about."

[16]So they hurried off and found Mary and Joseph, and the baby, who was lying in the manger. [17]When they had seen him, they spread the word concerning what had been told them about this child, [18]and all who heard it were amazed at what the shepherds said to them. [19]But Mary treasured up all these things and pondered them in her heart. [20]The shepherds returned, glorifying and praising God for all the things they had heard and seen, which were just as they had been told. (Luke 2:1-20)

The Messiah has been born! The angels delivered this much-anticipated announcement to lowly shepherds. Surprisingly, God chose to give the greatest news ever heard to humble men working in the fields. We can be thankful that God continues to reveal His Son today to all who are willing to accept Him.

5. How did God arrange the events of history to place Joseph and Mary in the right place at the right time?

a census to be taken of entire Roman world

6. What is the responsibility of those who discover the good news about Jesus?

Spread the word

How could you best share the truth of Christ's birth with a particular friend?

Reading the Bible

● ●

MARY AND JOSEPH BRING JESUS TO THE TEMPLE *Luke 2:21-40*

[21]On the eighth day, when it was time to circumcise him, he was named Jesus, the name the angel had given him before he had been conceived.

[22]When the time of their purification according to the Law of Moses had been completed, Joseph and Mary took him to Jerusalem to present him to the Lord [23](as it is written in the Law of the Lord, "Every firstborn male is to be consecrated to the Lord"), [24]and to offer a sacrifice in keeping with

what is said in the Law of the Lord: "a pair of doves or two young pigeons."

²⁵Now there was a man in Jerusalem called Simeon, who was righteous and devout. He was waiting for the consolation of Israel, and the Holy Spirit was upon him. ²⁶It had been revealed to him by the Holy Spirit that he would not die before he had seen the Lord's Christ. ²⁷Moved by the Spirit, he went into the temple courts. When the parents brought in the child Jesus to do for him what the custom of the Law required, ²⁸Simeon took him in his arms and praised God, saying:

²⁹"Sovereign Lord, as you have promised,
    you now dismiss your servant in peace.
³⁰For my eyes have seen your salvation,
    ³¹which you have prepared in the sight of all
        people,
³²a light for revelation to the Gentiles
    and for glory to your people Israel."

³³The child's father and mother marveled at what was said about him. ³⁴Then Simeon blessed them and said to Mary, his mother: "This child is destined to cause the falling and rising of many in Israel, and to be a sign that will be spoken against, ³⁵so that the thoughts of many hearts will be revealed. And a sword will pierce your own soul too."

³⁶There was also a prophetess, Anna, the daughter of Phanuel, of the tribe of Asher. She was very old; she had lived with her husband seven years after her marriage, ³⁷and then was a widow until she was eighty-four. She never left the temple but worshiped night and day, fasting and praying. ³⁸Coming up to them at that very moment, she gave thanks to God and spoke about the child to all who were looking forward to the redemption of Jerusalem.

³⁹When Joseph and Mary had done everything required by the Law of the Lord, they returned to Galilee to their own town of Nazareth. ⁴⁰And the child grew and became strong; he was filled with wisdom, and the grace of God was upon him.
(Luke 2:21-40)

Circumcision, an important Jewish ceremony, was performed soon after a son's birth. Joseph and Mary obeyed the law by circumcising Jesus, even though He was God's Son. Jesus fulfilled the requirements of God's law perfectly in every way.

7. How did Simeon and Anna each accept the baby Jesus?

Praising & Thanking - Rejoice!

How do you plan to follow the examples of Simeon and Anna?

8. What character traits were apparent in Jesus during His childhood?

strong
wise
grace of God upon him

thru april 13

VISITORS ARRIVE FROM EASTERN LANDS
Matthew 2:1-12

¹After Jesus was born in Bethlehem in Judea, during the time of King Herod, Magi from the east came to Jerusalem ²and asked, "Where is the one who has been born king of the Jews? We saw his star in the east and have come to worship him."

³When King Herod heard this he was disturbed, and all Jerusalem with him. ⁴When he had called together all the people's chief priests and teachers of the law, he asked them where the Christ was to be born. ⁵"In Bethlehem in Judea," they replied, "for this is what the prophet has written:

⁶"But you, Bethlehem, in the land of Judah,
*   are by no means least among the rulers of Judah;*
for out of you will come a ruler
*   who will be the shepherd of my people Israel."'*

⁷Then Herod called the Magi secretly and found out from them the exact time the star had appeared. ⁸He sent them to Bethlehem and said, "Go and make a careful search for the child. As soon as you find him, report to me, so that I too may go and worship him."

⁹After they had heard the king, they went on their way, and the star they had seen in the east went ahead of them until it stopped over the place where the child was. ¹⁰When they saw the star, they were overjoyed. ¹¹On coming to the house, they saw the child with his mother Mary, and they bowed down and worshiped him. Then they opened their treasures and presented him with gifts of gold and of incense and of myrrh. ¹²And having been warned in a dream not to go back to Herod, they returned to their country by another route. (Matthew 2:1-12)

The wise men are sometimes called *Magi*, meaning "great." These men traveled thousands of miles to see the Messiah. They worshiped Jesus because they believed He was the King of Kings. Like the wise men, we should give Jesus the praise and adoration He deserves.

9. What prompted the Magi to search for Jesus?

What lesson have
you learned from
the example of the
wise men that you
could apply to
your daily life?

10. How did the Magi react when they realized
   they had found the Christ?

In what concrete
ways can you
demonstrate your
worship to Jesus?

• •

THE ESCAPE TO EGYPT AND RETURN
TO NAZARETH *Matthew 2:13-23*

¹³*When they had gone, an angel of the Lord
appeared to Joseph in a dream. "Get up," he said,
"take the child and his mother and escape to Egypt.
Stay there until I tell you, for Herod is going to
search for the child to kill him."*

¹⁴*So he got up, took the child and his mother
during the night and left for Egypt, ¹⁵where he
stayed until the death of Herod. And so was fulfilled what the Lord had said through the prophet:
"Out of Egypt I called my son."*

¹⁶*When Herod realized that he had been out-
witted by the Magi, he was furious, and he gave
orders to kill all the boys in Bethlehem and its
vicinity who were two years old and under, in*

37

accordance with the time he had learned from the Magi. ¹⁷*Then what was said through the prophet Jeremiah was fulfilled:*

¹⁸*"A voice is heard in Ramah,*
    weeping and great mourning,
Rachel weeping for her children
    and refusing to be comforted,
because they are no more."

¹⁹*After Herod died, an angel of the Lord appeared in a dream to Joseph in Egypt* ²⁰*and said, "Get up, take the child and his mother and go to the land of Israel, for those who were trying to take the child's life are dead."*
²¹*So he got up, took the child and his mother and went to the land of Israel.* ²²*But when he heard that Archelaus was reigning in Judea in place of his father Herod, he was afraid to go there. Having been warned in a dream, he withdrew to the district of Galilee,* ²³*and he went and lived in a town called Nazareth. So was fulfilled what was said through the prophets: "He will be called a Nazarene."* (Matthew 2:13-23)

Both God and Joseph were concerned because the safety of baby Jesus was threatened by King Herod. Egypt was the nearest place of safety for Joseph and his family. In this way, the infant was saved from the wrath of King Herod. This fulfilled the prophecy of Hosea: "When Israel was a child I loved him, and out of Egypt I called my son" (Hosea 11:1).

11. How did Joseph respond to the angel's warning?

12. Why is it important to obey God immediately?

13. In what ways can we see God working behind the scenes in the events of Jesus' childhood?

• •

JESUS' YOUTH
Luke 2:41-52

[41]Every year his parents went to Jerusalem for the Feast of the Passover. [42]When he was twelve years old, they went up to the Feast, according to the custom. [43]After the Feast was over, while his parents were returning home, the boy Jesus stayed behind in Jerusalem, but they were unaware of it. [44]Thinking he was in their company, they traveled on for a

day. Then they began looking for him among their relatives and friends. ⁴⁵When they did not find him, they went back to Jerusalem to look for him. ⁴⁶After three days they found him in the temple courts, sitting among the teachers, listening to them and asking them questions. ⁴⁷Everyone who heard him was amazed at his understanding and his answers. ⁴⁸When his parents saw him, they were astonished. His mother said to him, "Son, why have you treated us like this? Your father and I have been anxiously searching for you."

⁴⁹"Why were you searching for me?" he asked. "Didn't you know I had to be in my Father's house?" ⁵⁰But they did not understand what he was saying to them.

⁵¹Then he went down to Nazareth with them and was obedient to them. But his mother treasured all these things in her heart. ⁵²And Jesus grew in wisdom and stature, and in favor with God and men. (Luke 2:41-52)

The Gospels are silent regarding incidents in Jesus' life between His return from Egypt and His baptism at age thirty, except for this account of His visit to the temple when He was twelve years old. This silence further emphasizes that the Gospels are a history of the Savior, not a biography of Jesus of Nazareth.

14. How is Jesus' response to His parents significant?

In what way should you strive to grow in wisdom and stature and in favor with God and others?

15. In what ways was Jesus' youth normal?

16. How was it extraordinary?

In what ways can you renew your enthusiasm for the message of Jesus' birth?

The shepherds and wise men were thrilled to hear the good news that the Christ had been born. When they finally found Him, they responded with joy, worship, and gifts. Christ is also worthy of the best *we* have to give Him. Worship Jesus for who He is—the Son of God.

INVITE A FRIEND!

God chose **John the Baptist** to become the prophet of whom Malachi had written, "Behold, I am going to send My messenger, and he will clear the way before Me" (Malachi 3:1, NASB). Before Jesus began His public ministry, John appeared out of the wilderness boldly proclaiming a unique message of repentance. God has given us a similar purpose—He wants us to point others to Christ. This lesson will show you how to follow John's example by inviting your friends to meet Jesus.

A voice of one calling: "In the desert prepare the way for the LORD; make straight in the wilderness a highway for our God." (Isaiah 40:3)

JOHN THE BAPTIST PREPARES THE WAY FOR JESUS *Matthew 3:1-12, Mark 1:2-8, Luke 3:1-20, John 1:19-28*

¹In the fifteenth year of the reign of Tiberius Caesar—when Pontius Pilate was governor of Judea, Herod tetrarch of Galilee, his brother Philip tetrarch of Iturea and Traconitis, and Lysanias tetrarch of Abilene—²during the high priesthood of Annas and Caiaphas, the word of God came to John son of Zechariah in the desert. ³He went into all the country around the Jordan, preaching a baptism of repentance for the forgiveness of sins. ⁴As is written in the book of the words of Isaiah the prophet:

"A voice of one calling in the desert,
'Prepare the way for the Lord,
    make straight paths for him.
⁵Every valley shall be filled in,
    every mountain and hill made low.
The crooked roads shall become straight,
    the rough ways smooth.
⁶And all mankind will see God's salvation.'"

⁷John said to the crowds coming out to be baptized by him, "You brood of vipers! Who warned you to flee from the coming wrath? ⁸Produce fruit in keeping with repentance. And do not begin to say to yourselves, 'We have Abraham as our father.' For I tell you that out of these stones God can raise up children for Abraham. ⁹The ax is already at the root of the trees, and every tree that does not produce good fruit will be cut down and thrown into the fire."

¹⁰"What should we do then?" the crowd asked.

¹¹John answered, "The man with two tunics should share with him who has none, and the one who has food should do the same."

¹²Tax collectors also came to be baptized. "Teacher," they asked, "what should we do?"

¹³"Don't collect any more than you are required to," he told them.

¹⁴Then some soldiers asked him, "And what should we do?"

He replied, "Don't extort money and don't accuse people falsely—be content with your pay."

¹⁵The people were waiting expectantly and were all wondering in their hearts if John might possibly be the Christ. ¹⁶John answered them all, "I baptize you with water. But one more powerful than I will come, the thongs of whose sandals I am not worthy to untie. He will baptize you with the Holy Spirit and with fire. ¹⁷His winnowing fork is in his hand to clear his threshing floor and to gather the wheat into his barn, but he will burn up the chaff with unquenchable fire." ¹⁸And with many other words John exhorted the people and preached the good news to them.

[19]But when John rebuked Herod the tetrarch because of Herodias, his brother's wife, and all the other evil things he had done, [20]Herod added this to them all: He locked John up in prison.
(Luke 3:1-20)

John fulfilled his role as the Messiah's forerunner by telling the people of his day to repent and seek God. People were moved by the truth of his words — many turned from their sin and were baptized. Before we can follow John's example by challenging others to change, we must demonstrate the fruits of repentance in our own lives.

  1. According to John, how can we prepare ourselves for Christ's return?

  2. How would you define true repentance?

In what area of
your life would
you like to see
the fruits of
repentance?

3. What often keeps us from repentance?

● ●

JOHN BAPTIZES JESUS
*Matthew 3:13-17, Mark 1:9-11, Luke 3:21-22,
John 1:29-34*

*[13]Then Jesus came from Galilee to the Jordan to be
baptized by John. [14]But John tried to deter him, saying, "I need to be baptized by you, and do you
come to me?"*

*[15]Jesus replied, "Let it be so now; it is proper
for us to do this to fulfill all righteousness." Then
John consented.*

*[16]As soon as Jesus was baptized, he went up out
of the water. At that moment heaven was opened,
and he saw the Spirit of God descending like a
dove and lighting on him. [17]And a voice from
heaven said, "This is my Son, whom I love; with
him I am well pleased." (Matthew 3:13-17)*

John the Baptist never imagined his first
encounter with the Messiah would be like this!
John knew that Jesus' baptism would be much
greater than his, yet Jesus came to him to be
baptized. Jesus reassured John that His baptism
would "fulfill all righteousness." God's Son did
not need to repent of sin, but He demonstrated
humble obedience to the Father through
baptism.

4. What mixed feelings do you think John had about baptizing Jesus?

5. How did the Father show His approval of Jesus' actions?

In what area of your life do you need to submit humbly to God's authority?

6. What message do we send to the world when we are baptized?

SATAN TEMPTS JESUS IN THE DESERT
Matthew 4:1-11, Mark 1:12-13, Luke 4:1-13

¹Then Jesus was led by the Spirit into the desert to be tempted by the devil. ²After fasting forty days and forty nights, he was hungry. ³The tempter came to him and said, "If you are the Son of God, tell these stones to become bread."

⁴Jesus answered, "It is written: 'Man does not live on bread alone, but on every word that comes from the mouth of God.'"

⁵Then the devil took him to the holy city and had him stand on the highest point of the temple. ⁶"If you are the Son of God," he said, "throw yourself down. For it is written:

"'He will command his angels concerning you,
*   and they will lift you up in their hands,*
so that you will not strike your foot against a
*   stone.'"*

⁷Jesus answered him, "It is also written: 'Do not put the Lord your God to the test.'"

⁸Again, the devil took him to a very high mountain and showed him all the kingdoms of the world and their splendor. ⁹"All this I will give you," he said, "if you will bow down and worship me."

¹⁰Jesus said to him, "Away from me, Satan! For it is written: 'Worship the Lord your God, and serve him only.'"

¹¹Then the devil left him, and angels came and attended him. (Matthew 4:1-11)

Immediately following Jesus' baptism, the Holy Spirit led Him into the desert to be confronted by Satan. The next forty days became an intense period of testing during which Jesus showed He was the perfect Son of God, able to withstand temptation and overcome the Devil. We can imitate Christ's perfect example when we feel vulnerable to temptation.

7. Why was Jesus especially vulnerable during this time?

8. What techniques does Satan use to entice us to sin?

9. How had Jesus prepared Himself to face these temptations?

What concrete
steps can you take
today to prepare
yourself to with-
stand temptation
in the future?

10. When do you feel most susceptible to
    temptation?

11. What can we learn from Jesus about facing
    and overcoming temptation?

• •

THE FIRST DISCIPLES FOLLOW JESUS
John 1:35-51

[35]*The next day John was there again with two of his
disciples.* [36]*When he saw Jesus passing by, he said,
"Look, the Lamb of God!"*

[37]*When the two disciples heard him say this,
they followed Jesus.* [38]*Turning around, Jesus saw
them following and asked, "What do you want?"*

*They said, "Rabbi" (which means Teacher),
"where are you staying?"*

[39]*"Come," he replied, "and you will see."*

So they went and saw where he was staying, and spent that day with him. It was about the tenth hour. *⁴⁰Andrew, Simon Peter's brother, was one of the two who heard what John had said and who had followed Jesus. ⁴¹The first thing Andrew did was to find his brother Simon and tell him, "We have found the Messiah" (that is, the Christ). ⁴²And he brought him to Jesus.*

Jesus looked at him and said, "You are Simon son of John. You will be called Cephas" (which, when translated, is Peter).

⁴³The next day Jesus decided to leave for Galilee. Finding Philip, he said to him, "Follow me."

⁴⁴Philip, like Andrew and Peter, was from the town of Bethsaida. ⁴⁵Philip found Nathanael and told him, "We have found the one Moses wrote about in the Law, and about whom the prophets also wrote—Jesus of Nazareth, the son of Joseph."

⁴⁶"Nazareth! Can anything good come from there?" Nathanael asked.

"Come and see," said Philip.

⁴⁷When Jesus saw Nathanael approaching, he said of him, "Here is a true Israelite, in whom there is nothing false."

⁴⁸"How do you know me?" Nathanael asked.

Jesus answered, "I saw you while you were still under the fig tree before Philip called you."

⁴⁹Then Nathanael declared, "Rabbi, you are the Son of God; you are the King of Israel."

⁵⁰Jesus said, "You believe because I told you I saw you under the fig tree. You shall see greater things than that." ⁵¹He then added, "I tell you the truth, you shall see heaven open, and the angels of God ascending and descending on the Son of Man." (John 1:35-51)

When Jesus began His public ministry, John introduced Him to some of his own disciples, who then followed Christ. John willingly retreated to the shadows so that Jesus could be in the spotlight. God desires this kind of humble service from all of us.

12. What does it mean to follow Jesus?

13. What attracts people to Jesus today? What attracted you to Him?

Which of your friends or family members would you like to introduce to Christ this week?

14. What fears keep us from telling our friends about Jesus?

15. How can we overcome these fears?

God did not call John to an easy life! He lived in the desert, nourished by locusts and wild honey. His bold message of repentance convinced some to change their sinful ways, but others responded with resentment and hatred. John gave up everything—even his life—to introduce Christ to the world. Showing our friends the way to Jesus may require personal sacrifice, but the eternal rewards are worth the cost.

What changes do you need to make in your lifestyle to become a more effective witness for Christ?

L E S S O N   F I V E
IN THE PUBLIC EYE

Jesus had been living in obscurity as a carpenter in Nazareth, but He caused quite a stir when He finally began His public ministry! Jesus won the allegiance of His disciples with His first miracle—turning water into wine. His actions in the temple courts during Passover got the attention of the most powerful religious leaders of that day. This lesson will help you understand how these early events in Jesus' ministry show that He is indeed the Son of God.

> "Then suddenly the Lord you are seeking will come to his temple; the messenger of the covenant, whom you desire, will come," says the LORD Almighty. (Malachi 3:1)

JESUS TURNS WATER INTO WINE
John 2:1-11

¹*On the third day a wedding took place at Cana in Galilee. Jesus' mother was there,* ²*and Jesus and his disciples had also been invited to the wedding.* ³*When the wine was gone, Jesus' mother said to him, "They have no more wine."*

⁴*"Dear woman, why do you involve me?" Jesus replied. "My time has not yet come."*

⁵*His mother said to the servants, "Do whatever he tells you."*

⁶*Nearby stood six stone water jars, the kind used by the Jews for ceremonial washing, each holding from twenty to thirty gallons.*

7Jesus said to the servants, "Fill the jars with water"; so they filled them to the brim.

8Then he told them, "Now draw some out and take it to the master of the banquet."

They did so, 9and the master of the banquet tasted the water that had been turned into wine. He did not realize where it had come from, though the servants who had drawn the water knew. Then he called the bridegroom aside 10and said, "Everyone brings out the choice wine first and then the cheaper wine after the guests have had too much to drink; but you have saved the best till now."

11This, the first of his miraculous signs, Jesus performed at Cana in Galilee. He thus revealed his glory, and his disciples put their faith in him. (John 2:1-11)

Jesus performed His first miracle at a wedding feast in Cana of Galilee. This miracle showed that Christ had power over nature and would use His divine authority to help others. The Gospel writer tells us that when Jesus' disciples saw Him turn water into wine, they believed that He really was the Messiah.

What problem do you need to surrender to Jesus today?

1. What problem did Mary face in this story? How did she deal with it?

Embarrasment to provide proper hospitality.

Jesus mother informed Jesus.

and Jesus turned water to wine. 1st miracle

2. Why did Jesus perform this miracle?

revealed his glory so disciples would have faith

3. How does Jesus Christ reveal Himself to us today?

Prayer – holy spirit

4. What can we learn from the example set by the disciples in this passage?

Faith

How could you demonstrate your trust in Christ's power this next week?

JESUS CLEARS THE TEMPLE
John 2:12-25

¹²*After this he went down to Capernaum with his mother and brothers and his disciples. There they stayed for a few days.*

¹³*When it was almost time for the Jewish Passover, Jesus went up to Jerusalem.* ¹⁴*In the temple courts he found men selling cattle, sheep and doves, and others sitting at tables exchanging money.* ¹⁵*So he made a whip out of cords, and drove all from the temple area, both sheep and cattle; he scattered the coins of the money changers and overturned their tables.* ¹⁶*To those who sold doves he said, "Get these out of here! How dare you turn my Father's house into a market!"*

¹⁷*His disciples remembered that it is written: "Zeal for your house will consume me."*

¹⁸*Then the Jews demanded of him, "What miraculous sign can you show us to prove your authority to do all this?"*

¹⁹*Jesus answered them, "Destroy this temple, and I will raise it again in three days."*

²⁰*The Jews replied, "It has taken forty-six years to build this temple, and you are going to raise it in three days?"* ²¹*But the temple he had spoken of was his body.* ²²*After he was raised from the dead, his disciples recalled what he had said. Then they believed the Scripture and the words that Jesus had spoken.*

²³*Now while he was in Jerusalem at the Passover Feast, many people saw the miraculous signs he was doing and believed in his name.* ²⁴*But Jesus would not entrust himself to them, for he knew all men.* ²⁵*He did not need man's testimony about man, for he knew what was in a man.* (John 2:12-25)

Jewish families from all over the world traveled to Jerusalem to celebrate Passover. Because these out-of-town visitors needed to exchange their foreign coins to give their offerings, money-changers crowded their way into the temple courts to take advantage of the situation. The greed and dishonesty of the merchants infuriated Jesus. He could not allow so many people to make a mockery of His Father's house.

5. What do Jesus' actions reveal about His nature?

6. What impact do you think Jesus' actions had on the people present?

7. In what ways do we use church for our own advantage?

How do you need
to change your
attitude toward
church?

8. How can we guard against misusing God's house?

• •

NICODEMUS VISITS JESUS AT NIGHT
John 3:1-21

¹Now there was a man of the Pharisees named Nicodemus, a member of the Jewish ruling council. ²He came to Jesus at night and said, "Rabbi, we know you are a teacher who has come from God. For no one could perform the miraculous signs you are doing if God were not with him."

³In reply Jesus declared, "I tell you the truth, no one can see the kingdom of God unless he is born again."

⁴"How can a man be born when he is old?" Nicodemus asked. "Surely he cannot enter a second time into his mother's womb to be born!"

⁵Jesus answered, "I tell you the truth, no one can enter the kingdom of God unless he is born of water and the Spirit. ⁶Flesh gives birth to flesh, but the Spirit gives birth to spirit. ⁷You should not be surprised at my saying, 'You must be born again.' ⁸The wind blows wherever it pleases. You hear its sound, but you cannot tell where it comes from or where it is going. So it is with everyone born of the Spirit."

⁹"How can this be?" Nicodemus asked.

¹⁰"You are Israel's teacher," said Jesus, "and do you not understand these things? ¹¹I tell you the truth, we speak of what we know, and we testify to what we have seen, but still you people do not accept our testimony. ¹²I have spoken to you of earthly things and you do not believe; how then will you believe if I speak of heavenly things? [13]No one has ever gone into heaven except the one who came from heaven—the Son of Man. [14]Just as Moses lifted up the snake in the desert, so the Son of Man must be lifted up, [15]that everyone who believes in him may have eternal life.

[16]"For God so loved the world that he gave his one and only Son, that whoever believes in him shall not perish but have eternal life. [17]For God did not send his Son into the world to condemn the world, but to save the world through him. [18]Whoever believes in him is not condemned, but whoever does not believe stands condemned already because he has not believed in the name of God's one and only Son. [19]This is the verdict: Light has come into the world, but men loved darkness instead of light because their deeds were evil. [20]Everyone who does evil hates the light, and will not come into the light for fear that his deeds will be exposed. [21]But whoever lives by the truth comes into the light, so that it may be seen plainly that what he has done has been done through God." (John 3:1-21)

Nicodemus, a rich and powerful man, approached Jesus seeking answers to his spiritual questions. As a member of the Sanhedrin, he had heard of—or maybe even seen first-hand—Jesus' audacious act of clearing the temple. He probably wanted to get the facts straight for himself. Jesus gave him a lot more than he expected—He challenged Nicodemus to be "born again"!

9. How would you explain to a friend what it means to be born again?

10. What did Nicodemus believe about Jesus?

How can you thank the Lord today for the gift of His Son?

11. How did Jesus explain to Nicodemus the way to enter the Kingdom of God?

12. How does this passage identify Jesus as the Son of God?

JOHN THE BAPTIST TELLS MORE ABOUT JESUS *John 3:22-36*

²²*After this, Jesus and his disciples went out into the Judean countryside, where he spent some time with them, and baptized.* ²³*Now John also was baptizing at Aenon near Salim, because there was plenty of water, and people were constantly coming to be baptized.* ²⁴*(This was before John was put in prison.)* ²⁵*An argument developed between some of John's disciples and a certain Jew over the matter of ceremonial washing.* ²⁶*They came to John and said to him, "Rabbi, that man who was with you on the other side of the Jordan—the one you testified about—well, he is baptizing, and everyone is going to him."*

²⁷*To this John replied, "A man can receive only what is given him from heaven.* ²⁸*You yourselves can testify that I said, 'I am not the Christ but am sent ahead of him.'* ²⁹*The bride belongs to the bridegroom. The friend who attends the bridegroom waits and listens for him, and is full of joy when he hears the bridegroom's voice. That joy is mine, and it is now complete.* ³⁰*He must become greater; I must become less.*

³¹*"The one who comes from above is above all; the one who is from the earth belongs to the earth, and speaks as one from the earth. The one who comes from heaven is above all.* ³²*He testifies to what he has seen and heard, but no one accepts his testimony.* ³³*The man who has accepted it has certified that God is truthful.* ³⁴*For the one whom God has sent speaks the words of God, for God gives the Spirit without limit.* ³⁵*The Father loves the Son and has placed everything in his hands.* ³⁶*Whoever believes in the Son has eternal life, but whoever rejects the Son will not see life, for God's wrath remains on him."* (John 3:22-36)

After the Passover, Jesus and His disciples began to minister in the Judean countryside, the same area in which John and his disciples were working. John's disciples became jealous because so many people were going to Jesus to be baptized. John explained that it was only right for Jesus' following to grow and his to decrease. Clearly, John cared more about telling the truth about Jesus than his own popularity.

What steps can you take to give Jesus more prominence in your life?

13. What reasons did John give for the growth of Jesus' ministry over his own?

14. What does John's explanation teach us about who Jesus is?

What difference should the knowledge that Jesus is the Son of God make in your everyday life?

15. What lessons can we learn from John's attitude?

Only John's Gospel records these events in Jesus' early ministry. In keeping with his objective, and under the guidance of the Holy Spirit, John included these stories because they help show that Jesus is who He said He is—the Son of God. If we choose to believe this fact, it will change the way we live!

HARMONY OF THE LIFE AND MINISTRY OF JESUS CHRIST

	MATTHEW	MARK	LUKE	JOHN
	THE BEGINNING			

LESSON 1

	MATTHEW	MARK	LUKE	JOHN
The men who wrote the Gospels		1:1	1:1-4	
God became a human being				1:1-18
The ancestors of Jesus	1:1-17		3:23-38	

LESSON 2

	MATTHEW	MARK	LUKE	JOHN
An angel promises the birth of John to Zechariah			1:5-25	
An angel promises the birth of Jesus to Mary			1:26-38	
Mary visits Elizabeth			1:39-56	
John the Baptist is born			1:57-80	

LESSON 3

	MATTHEW	MARK	LUKE	JOHN
An angel appears to Joseph	1:18-25			
Jesus is born			2:1-20	
Mary and Joseph bring Jesus to the temple			2:21-40	
Visitors arrive from eastern lands	2:1-12			
The escape to Egypt and return to Nazareth	2:13-23			
Jesus' youth			2:41-52	

LESSON 4

	MATTHEW	MARK	LUKE	JOHN
John the Baptist prepares the way for Jesus	3:1-12	1:2-8	3:1-20	1:19-28
John baptizes Jesus	3:13-17	1:9-11	3:21-22	1:29-34
Satan tempts Jesus in the desert	4:1-11	1:12-13	4:1-13	
The first disciples follow Jesus				1:35-51

	MATTHEW	MARK	LUKE	JOHN
LESSON 5	*Jesus turns water into wine*			2:1-11
	Jesus clears the temple			2:12-25
	Nicodemus visits Jesus at night			3:1-21
	John the Baptist tells more about Jesus			3:22-36

CHALLENGING TRADITION

	MATTHEW	MARK	LUKE	JOHN
LESSON 1	*The Samaritan woman believes in Jesus*			4:1-42
	Jesus preaches in Galilee 4:12	1:14-15	4:14-15	4:43-45
	Jesus heals a government official's son			4:46-54
	Jesus is rejected at Nazareth		4:16-30	
LESSON 2	*Jesus moves to Capernaum* 4:13-17		4:31	
	Four fisherman follow Jesus 4:18-22	1:16-20	5:1-11	
	Jesus heals and teaches people 4:23-25; 8:1-4,14-17; 9:1-8	1:21–2:12	4:33-44, 5:12-26	
	Jesus eats with sinners at Matthew's house 9:9-13	2:13-17	5:27-32	
LESSON 3	*Religious leaders ask Jesus about fasting* 9:14-17	2:18-22	5:33-39	
	Jesus heals people on the Sabbath 12:1-21	2:23–3:12	6:1-11	5:1-47
	Jesus selects the twelve disciples 10:2-4	3:13-19	6:12-16	
	Jesus gives the Beatitudes 5:1-16		6:17-26	
	Jesus teaches about the law 5:17-48		6:27-36	

	MATTHEW	MARK	LUKE	JOHN
LESSON 4	*Jesus teaches about giving and prayer* 6:1-8, 6:16–7:12		6:37-42	
	Jesus teaches about the way to Heaven 7:13-29		6:43-49	
	A Roman centurion demonstrates faith 8:5-13		7:1-10	
	Jesus raises a widow's son from the dead		7:11-17	
LESSON 5	*Jesus eases John's doubt* 11:1-30		7:18-35	
	A sinful woman anoints Jesus' feet		7:36–8:3	
	Religious leaders falsely accuse Jesus 12:22-45	3:20-30	11:14-28	
	Jesus describes His true family 12:46-50	3:31-35	8:19-21	
	THE MESSIAH			
LESSON 1	*Jesus teaches through parables* 13:1-52	4:1-34	8:4-18	
	Jesus calms the storm 8:23-27	4:35-41	8:22-25	
	Jesus sends the demons into a herd of pigs 8:28-34	5:1-20	8:26-39	
	Jesus heals people and raises a girl to life 9:18-34	5:21-43	8:40-56	
LESSON 2	*The people of Nazareth refuse to believe* 13:53-58	6:1-6		
	Jesus sends out the twelve disciples 9:35–10:42	6:7-13	9:1-6	
	Herod kills John the Baptist 14:1-12	6:14-29	9:7-9	
	Jesus feeds the five thousand 14:13-21	6:30-44	9:10-17	6:1-15

	MATTHEW	MARK	LUKE	JOHN
LESSON 3	Jesus walks on water			
	14:22-36	6:45-56		6:16-21
	Jesus is the true bread from Heaven			
				6:22-71
	Jesus teaches about inner purity			
	15:1-20	7:1-23		
	Jesus sends a demon out of a girl			
	15:21-28	7:24-30		
	Jesus feeds four thousand			
	15:29-39	7:31–8:10		
LESSON 4	Religious leaders ask for a sign in the sky			
	16:1-12	8:11-21		
	Jesus restores sight to a blind man			
		8:22-26		
	Peter says Jesus is the Messiah			
	16:13-20	8:27-30	9:18-20	
	Jesus predicts His death the first time			
	16:21-28	8:31–9:1	9:21-27	
LESSON 5	Jesus is transfigured on the mountain			
	17:1-13	9:2-13	9:28-36	
	Jesus heals a demon-possessed boy			
	17:14-21	9:14-29	9:37-43	
	Jesus predicts His death the second time			
	17:22-23	9:30-32	9:44-45	
	Peter finds the coin in the fish's mouth			
	17:24-27			

FOLLOWING JESUS

	MATTHEW	MARK	LUKE	JOHN
LESSON 1	Jesus warns against temptation			
	18:1-35	9:33-50	9:46-50	
	Jesus teaches about the cost of following Him			
	8:18-22,	10:1	9:51-62	7:2-9
	19:1-2			
	Jesus teaches openly at the temple			
				7:10-53
LESSON 2	Jesus forgives an adulterous woman			
				8:1-11
	Jesus teaches about Himself			
				8:12-59
	Jesus heals a blind man			
				9:1-41

	MATTHEW	MARK	LUKE	JOHN
LESSON 3	Jesus is the good shepherd			10:1-21
	Jesus sends out seventy-two messengers		10:1-24	
	Jesus tells the parable of the good Samaritan		10:25-37	
	Jesus visits Mary and Martha		10:38-42	
LESSON 4	Jesus teaches His disciples about prayer 6:9-15		11:1-13	
	Jesus exposes the religious leaders		11:37–12:12	
	Jesus warns the people		12:13–13:21	
	Religious leaders surround Jesus at the temple			10:22-42
LESSON 5	Jesus heals and teaches people		13:22–14:24	
	Jesus teaches about the cost of being a disciple		14:25-35	
	Jesus tells three parables		15:1-32	
	ANSWERING THE CALL			
LESSON 1	Jesus teaches His disciples		16:1–17:10	
	Jesus raises Lazarus from the dead			11:1-44
	Jesus heals ten men with leprosy		17:11-19	
LESSON 2	Jesus teaches about the Kingdom of God		17:20-37	
	Jesus tells two parables on prayer		18:1-14	
	Jesus teaches about marriage and divorce 19:3-12	10:2-12		
	Jesus blesses little children 19:13-15	10:13-16	18:15-17	

	MATTHEW	MARK	LUKE	JOHN
LESSON 3	*Jesus speaks to the rich young man* 19:16–20:16	10:17-31	18:18-30	
	Jesus teaches about serving others 20:17-28	10:32-45	18:31-34	
	Jesus heals a blind beggar 20:29-34	10:46-52	18:35-43	
LESSON 4	*Jesus brings salvation to Zacchaeus's home*		19:1-10	
	Jesus tells the parable of the king's ten servants		19:11-27	
	Religious leaders plot to kill Jesus			11:45-57, 12:9-11
	Jesus rides into Jerusalem on a donkey 21:1-11,14-17	11:1-11	19:28-44	12:12-13
LESSON 5	*Jesus curses the fig tree* 21:18-19	11:12-14		
	Jesus clears the temple again 21:12-13	11:15-19	19:45-48	
	Jesus summarizes His purpose and message			12:20-50
	Jesus says His disciples can pray for anything 21:20-22	11:20-25		
	FINAL TEACHINGS			
LESSON 1	*Religious leaders challenge Jesus' authority* 21:23-27	11:27-33	20:1-8	
	Jesus tells three parables 21:28–22:14	12:1-12	20:9-19	
	Religious leaders ask Jesus three questions 22:15-40	12:13-34	20:20-40	
	Religious leaders cannot answer Jesus' question 22:41-46	12:35-37	20:41-44	
LESSON 2	*Jesus warns against the religious leaders* 23:1-12	12:38-40	20:45-47	
	Jesus condemns the religious leaders 23:13-39			
	A poor widow gives all she has	12:41-44	21:1-4	
	Jesus tells about the future 24:1-51	13:1-37	21:5-38	

	MATTHEW	MARK	LUKE	JOHN
LESSON 3	Jesus tells about the final judgment 25:1-46			
	Religious leaders plot to kill Jesus 26:1-5	14:1-2	22:1-2	
	A woman anoints Jesus with perfume 26:6-13	14:3-9		12:1-8
	Judas agrees to betray Jesus 26:14-16	14:10-11	22:3-6	
LESSON 4	Disciples prepare for the Passover 26:17-19	14:12-16	22:7-13	
	Jesus washes His disciples' feet			13:1-20
	Jesus foretells His betrayal and suffering 26:20-25	14:17-21	22:14-16,21-30	13:21-30
LESSON 5	Jesus and His disciples have the Last Supper 26:26-28	14:22-24	22:17-20	
	Jesus talks with His disciples about the future 26:29-30	14:25-26		13:31–14:31
	Jesus predicts Peter's denial 26:31-35	14:27-31	22:31-38	
	Jesus teaches about the vine and the branches			15:1–16:4
	THE CROSS AND THE RESURRECTION			
LESSON 1	Jesus teaches about the Holy Spirit and prayer			16:5-33
	Jesus prays for Himself and believers			17:1-26
	Jesus agonizes in the garden 26:36-46	14:32-42	22:39-46	18:1
	Jesus is betrayed and arrested 26:47-56	14:43-52	22:47-53	18:2-11
LESSON 2	Jesus is questioned and condemned 26:57,59-68, 27:1	14:53,55-65, 15:1	22:54,63-71	18:12-14,19-24
	Peter denies knowing Jesus 26:58,69-75	14:54,66-72	22:54-62	18:15-18,25-27
	Judas kills himself (see also Acts 1:18-19) 27:3-10			
	Jesus stands trial before Pilate and Herod 27:2,11-31	15:1-20	23:1-25	18:28–19:16

	MATTHEW	MARK	LUKE	JOHN
LESSON 3	Jesus is crucified			
	27:31-56	15:20-41	23:26-49	19:16-37
	Jesus is buried			
	27:57-66	15:42-47	23:50-56	19:38-42
	Jesus rises from the dead and appears to the women			
	28:1-15	16:1-11	24:1-12	20:1-18
LESSON 4	Jesus appears to two believers traveling on the road			
		16:12-13	24:13-35	
	Jesus appears to the disciples behind locked doors			
		16:14	24:36-43	20:19-23
	Jesus appears to the disciples, including Thomas			
				20:24-31
	Jesus appears to the disciples while fishing			
				21:1-25
LESSON 5	Jesus gives the Great Commission			
	28:16-20	16:15-18		
	Jesus appears to the disciples in Jerusalem (see also Acts 1:3-8)			
			24:44-49	
	Jesus ascends into Heaven (see also Acts 1:9-12)			
		16:19-20	24:50-53	

BIBLE STUDIES AND SMALL-GROUP MATERIALS FROM NAVPRESS

BIBLE STUDY SERIES
Design for Discipleship
Foundation for Christian Living
God in You
Learning to Love
The Life and Ministry of
     Jesus Christ
LifeChange
Love One Another
Pilgrimage Guides
Radical Relationships
Studies in Christian Living
Thinking Through Discipleship

TOPICAL BIBLE STUDIES
Becoming a Woman of Excellence
Becoming a Woman of Freedom
Becoming a Woman of Prayer
Becoming a Woman of Purpose
The Blessing Study Guide
Celebrating Life!
Growing in Christ
Growing Strong in God's Family
Homemaking
Husbands and Wives
Intimacy with God
Jesus Cares for Women
Jesus Changes Women
Lessons on Assurance
Lessons on Christian Living
Loving Your Husband
Loving Your Wife
A Mother's Legacy
Parents and Children
Praying from God's Heart
Strategies for a Successful
     Marriage
Surviving Life in the Fast Lane
To Run and Not Grow Tired
To Stand and Not Be Moved
To Walk and Not Grow Weary

What God Does When Men Pray
When the Squeeze is On

BIBLE STUDIES WITH COMPANION BOOKS
Bold Love
Daughters of Eve
The Discipline of Grace
The Feminine Journey
From Bondage to Bonding
Hiding from Love
Inside Out
The Masculine Journey
The Practice of Godliness
The Pursuit of Holiness
Secret Longings of the Heart
Spiritual Disciplines for the
     Christian Life
Tame Your Fears
Transforming Grace
Trusting God
What Makes a Man?

SMALL-GROUP RESOURCES
201 Great Questions
Discipleship Journal's 101 Best
     Small-Group Ideas
How to Build a Small-Groups
     Ministry
How to Have Great Small-Group
     Meetings
How to Lead Small Groups
The Navigator Bible Studies
     Handbook
New Testament LessonMaker
The Small-Group Leaders
     Training Course

NAVPRESS ◐
BRINGING TRUTH TO LIFE
www.navpress.org

Get your copies today at your local Christian bookstore, or call
(800) 366-7788 and ask for offer **NPBS**.